Original title:
The Window of Tomorrow

Copyright © 2025 Creative Arts Management OÜ
All rights reserved.

Author: Cameron Blair
ISBN HARDBACK: 978-1-80587-187-3
ISBN PAPERBACK: 978-1-80587-657-1

Lighthouses of Hope

In a world filled with jigsaw gaps,
We search for clues, and maybe maps.
Each lighthouse beams a quirky light,
Guiding us home through day and night.

A seagull squawks, 'You missed the boat!',
While jellyfish dance, 'Hey, take note!'
In laughter, we find our silly way,
As waves of fortune crash and sway.

Pathways Through the Unknown

We wander paths where shadows play,
Each twist and turn, a chance to sway.
A squirrel offers life advice,
While lost socks debate their price.

Each step ahead, a comic quest,
With tumbleweeds, we jest and jest.
In the forest of chance we grin,
For every loss, there's likely win.

Fragments of Possible Realities

In my mind, a world of glee,
Where cats wear hats and dance with bees.
The clock strikes twelve—they just won't stop,
While pizza steals the last cookie top.

With dreams in bits, and whims on cue,
I spot a hamster in my shoe.
He winks at me, I laugh and spin,
In every chaos, there's joy within.

Sails of Future Winds

With paper boats, we drift away,
Through puddles bright, on a sunny day.
The breeze carries whispers and jokes,
As ducks pretend to be fine folks.

Each gust propels our silly dreams,
Where cotton candy rivers gleam.
With sails of laughter, we set course,
To futures bright, we find our force.

Prism of Tomorrow's Light

Rainbows dance in my glass frame,
Silly shadows joining the game.
What's that hue I see today?
Orange socks say, 'Let's play!'

Funky shapes flit to and fro,
Chasing giggles, quick and slow.
A floaty cat with a bowtie,
Waves hello as he floats by!

The Canvas Yet to Fill

Brush in hand, I splash away,
Colors pop, like kids at play.
Puppies painting rainbows bright,
Make a mess, oh what a sight!

Splattering dreams on a white slate,
A dancing penguin, isn't he great?
Swirls and twirls of chocolate dreams,
Painting joy, or so it seems!

Visions in the Mist

Fog rolls in, a playful tease,
Where's my hat? It's hard to see!
A bunny hops, then slips in mud,
Laughter floods like a cheerful flood!

Clouds whisper secrets up on high,
What's that shape? A pizza pie?
Wacky visions float in air,
A dancing bear with quite a flair!

The Future in Blossoms

Flowers giggle in the breeze,
Tickling noses, oh what a tease!
A daisy winks, 'Join the fun!'
Bumblebees hum, 'All is done!'

Petals burst in colors bright,
Laughing blossoms, what a sight!
'Let's grow higher!' roses shout,
While sleepy daisies dream about!

Colors of a New Day

Sunshine spills like orange juice,
Birds are singing loud and loose.
Dancing rays on waking grass,
Time to wear my silly mask.

Socks are mismatched, what a sight,
Waking dreams feel oh-so-right.
Coffee brews like bubbling stew,
I might just jump in with my shoe!

Bumblebees wear tiny hats,
Chasing butterflies and spats.
Tickled by a breezy nudge,
Nature grins, I can't judge.

Where Horizons Merge

Clouds wear coats of fluffy cream,
Wiggles in the sunlight beam.
Laughter echoes through the skies,
As squirrels juggle in disguise.

The sun trips on a sleepy hill,
Chasing shadows, what a thrill!
Every blade of grass takes part,
In this grand and goofy art.

Butterflies plot their grand parade,
In a dance that won't soon fade.
Today, I'll take a daring jump,
And land right in a muddy plump!

Gaze into the Horizon

As I peer across the bay,
I swear I heard a fish say "Hey!"
It wore a tie and bright blue shoes,
Stepping out to share the news.

Distant waves, a giggling sound,
A crab in shades, strutted around.
Seagulls racing, oh, so bold,
Chasing dreams where tales are told.

Raindrops plan a funny race,
Splashing puddles, what a place!
Together, we'll bounce and sway,
In the circle of this day!

Visions Beyond Glass

Through the pane, I see a goat,
Wearing boots and riding a boat.
With every bounce, it sings a tune,
Underneath the smiling moon.

Cats in ties are chasing light,
While raccoons dance with pure delight.
Gardens filled with dancing greens,
And mischievous tomato beans.

Frogs in bowler hats do cheer,
As they hop and leap from here!
Life outside is quite the show,
Filled with giggles and a glow!

The Clear Horizon

Horizon laughs as I peer out,
What's this? A squirrel's acrobatic route.
He spins and flips, a performance art,
While I spill coffee, trying to take part.

Balloons float by, just out of reach,
A kite's in a tangle; oh, what a breach!
The sun winks down, playing hide and seek,
And I just chortle at this funny peak.

Unfolding Hidden Pathways

Beneath my feet, a garden of dreams,
With mismatched socks, I'm lost in the seams.
A path of cookies? Count me in now!
I'll trip on the magic; I'll jump and I'll bow.

The hedges are whispering secrets of glee,
While I chase a butterfly, it's taunting me.
In a world where laughter paves all the streets,
Let's dance on the sidewalks in sparkly feats.

The Lure of New Skies

Clouds wearing hats, oh what a sight!
They bounce in the breeze, playful and light.
A rainbow slides into my coffee cup,
And I giggle as it rains colorful sup.

Birds wearing sunglasses sing silly tunes,
While I pull a face at the nearby raccoons.
They're plotting my snacks—oh, what a heist!
With each little prank, they just add to the feast.

The Brightness Yet to Be

Sunrise giggles, tickling my toes,
Shining like glitter, it sparkles and glows.
The world may be weird, but that's what I crave,
With jellybean paths, I feel like a knave.

Every moment spins into a fairytale,
Where smiles are currency, and dreams never pale.
With every hiccup, I'll take one more leap,
For laughter's the treasure my heart longs to keep.

Hopes in the First Light

With morning sun, I stretch my arm,
A fluff-pillow fight just feels like charm.
Coffee spills as I dream and giggle,
Oops! A splash makes the cat do a wiggle.

Just like a toast that's burnt on one side,
Life's little mishaps can't be denied.
I gaze out the frame with a cheeky grin,
Tomorrow's wild ride can finally begin!

Portals of Anticipation

Peeking through glass, I spy my plan,
To disco with squirrels, I'm a bold fan!
Balloons in the backyard, what a delight,
But wait, are those pigeons ready to fight?

Each morning's a stage, a dance quite absurd,
Where toast takes a leap like it's never heard.
I'll ride on a cloud, with a wink and a cheer,
And juggle my dreams like I've nothing to fear!

Dreams on the Breeze

Whispers of wind with a jovial tune,
Tickle the trees as I hum to the moon.
Kites zoom above in a crafty ballet,
While ducks on a scooter come out to play!

Pies in the sky, watch them swirl and twirl,
Each slice brings a giggle, a whirl and a swirl.
I laugh with the clouds, joking all day,
Who knew that tomorrow would come out to play?

Rays of Unseen Futures

Chasing the sunbeams, I trip and I fall,
My flip-flop has launched off, like it's got a call!
I laugh at my shadow, it's dancing with glee,
Winking at me from the old cherry tree.

Skateboard my dreams as the world spins fast,
With silly mess-ups, I'm free at last.
Tomorrow holds secrets in each golden spray,
And I'll be the jester, come what may!

A Doorway to Future Clouds

Through the door, I peek and stare,
Expecting unicorns in mid-air.
But all I find are socks and dust,
And little crumbs of yesterday's crust.

I knock on dreams, they giggle back,
With silly hats and a clownish track.
They juggle hopes like floating pies,
While I just ponder and tie my ties.

A leap of faith on tiles so bright,
Them hoping to land with all their might.
Instead I slip, I laugh, I roll,
Into a pile with a silly mole!

But through the chaos, there's a spark,
A cheeky laugh, a little lark.
For future clouds are soft and round,
And joy blooms brightly all around.

Reflections in the Morning Dew

Each droplet sings a funny tune,
While I dance with a wayward spoon.
The spider spins a tale of cheer,
As breakfast plans start to appear.

Reflection shows a silly fate,
A sleepy bear just can't be late.
With honey on the side, I grin,
And wonder where my socks have been.

The grass giggles as I trip,
And give my coffee cup a sip.
While butterflies dance, I can't resist,
This morning dew is quite the twist.

So here's to laughs and gleeful sighs,
With every dew drop that splashes, it flies.
The mirror winks, the sun peeks in,
Ready for chaotic fun to begin!

Ciphers of Celestial Visions

In a language made of cheesy lines,
Stars write secrets in whimsical signs.
I try to decode with a jelly bean,
But the message comes out all green and mean.

Aliens giggle from their far-off space,
Sipping soda at a silly pace.
They wave their antennas, shining bright,
As I hop along, a curious sight!

Comets throw confetti like it's a game,
While meteors wink, oh, what a name!
I scribble my hopes on a pancake slate,
As pancakes twirl and spin, oh, fate!

Navigating with a rubber duck,
To find the treasure of silly luck.
In ciphers full of laughter and sass,
I send my dreams into the cosmos vast.

Embracing What Lies Ahead

I stride with glee, my hair askew,
Pursuing dreams that feel quite new.
A wandering cat leads the way,
Winking at fate, come what may.

I reach for skies, with clouds in tow,
Chasing after a rainbow glow.
Instead I trip on a wayward shoe,
And land quite softly on a hopeful rue.

With a grin so wide, I dare to care,
As the wind whispers, 'Don't you dare spare!'
So here I jump with happy feet,
Embracing the future that's rather sweet.

A dance of mishaps, a comedy show,
With every turn, it's laughter I throw.
For what lies ahead is an endless spree,
Filled with fun, just wait and see!

Light Through the Pane

Sunlight spills, a silly prance,
Cats chase beams in a sunny dance,
Mom yells, 'Get off that flower pot!',
But the chase is on, why not?

Birds debate their morning song,
Who knew chirping could be wrong?
Squirrels plotting from the tree,
A nutty plan for a cup of tea!

Glasses clink in the warm air,
Lemonade spills, oh, that's unfair!
Kids giggle by the gravel path,
Creating chaos, doing math!

Frogs in pond, a joyful scene,
Jumping high, as if on a trampoline,
Each splash sends ripples to race,
Tomorrow's fun awaits in space!

Visions on the Breeze

A breezy thought floats by with flair,
Twirling leaves in the afternoon air,
Silly hats fly, who caught that?
A bird takes it, can you imagine that?

Dreams of cupcakes drift above,
Sprinkles rain, cravings we love,
"Is frosting a food group?" they jest,
As they munch and giggle, so blessed!

A kite soars, a rainbow swap,
Over the park, a sticky plop,
Cheese and crackers, a feast to share,
While ants march in, all unaware!

Bubbles float and dance in glee,
The world's a stage, can't you see?
Laughter echoes as friends unite,
In silly dreams of tomorrow's flight!

Portal to Tomorrow's Dreams

A door swings wide, a wobble and sway,
Socks and sandals begin their play,
"Where's my left foot?" a shout rings clear,
As mismatched pairs switch into gear!

Time ticks on in a jubilant race,
Frogs in bow ties, what a fine place,
They gather to argue, who hops the best,
In this crazy ribbiting jest!

Pancakes flip in the sunny spot,
Maple syrup's the secret plot,
Uncles wear wigs and dance like fools,
In this realm, all break the rules!

Tidal waves of giggles and glee,
Who knew tomorrow could be so... free?
With ducks in tutus, the sun sets slow,
Hoping this dream might steal the show!

The Lattice of Time

Twinkling stars in a woven net,
Who knew bedtime could be so set?
Pajamas dance around the floor,
As giggles waltz right out the door!

Pineapples wearing crowns of gold,
Tell tales of mischief, now they're bold,
"Where do we go?" they curiously hum,
To bake a cake that's fit for fun!

Each hour loops with a silly cheer,
With whispering shadows that volunteer,
To share the secrets of leapfrog leaps,
As bedtime promises chocolate peeps!

Through laughter's light, we wade and sway,
Tomorrow's treasures waiting to play,
So hold on tight with a wink and grin,
For this maze of nonsense is where we begin!

A View to Infinite Tomorrows

Peeking out to see the sun,
I wonder if today's the one.
Will the cat chase shadows wide?
Or will we both just stay inside?

With coffee brewing, oh so strong,
I think I'll sing a silly song.
The world outside is loud and bright,
But here I'll dance in fuzzy light.

Neighbors argue, dogs do bark,
I dodge the raindrops, miss the mark.
In pajamas, I take a stroll,
To see if today's less dull than coal.

So here's my toast to future days,
Creating now in silly ways.
Just like a kid with toys to throw,
Tomorrow's laugh is what I know.

Moments yet to be Caught

I set my sights on flying high,
With plans to tickle clouds in sky.
Each moment sparkles, like confetti,
This life is sweet, and yet quite messy.

I chase my cat around the room,
While plotting my next day's grand bloom.
Success or fail, who really knows?
My only goal? To dodge the toes!

A sandwich here, a nap right there,
With dreams that float like vintage air.
Will I trip on my own two feet?
A laugh a day makes it all sweet!

So catch me now while I'm still bold,
Tomorrow's stories will unfold.
With giggles echoing all around,
In life's sweet chaos, joy is found.

The Doorway to Endless Sky

I opened wide my door today,
And let the sunshine come to play.
The dust bunnies danced, oh what a sight,
Even my shoes started a fight!

Birds chirped gossip from the tree,
As if they knew, just wait and see.
They eye my breakfast on the porch,
With hopes my toast is worth the search.

I'll build a kite from old junk mail,
And send it soaring without fail.
If it wraps 'round a branch, who cares?
The sky's my friend; we'll trade some stares.

So here's to whimsies yet unseen,
To laughter spilling bright and keen.
That door is wide, let's dance and fly,
Tomorrow's treasures, oh my, oh my!

Horizon's Call

With one foot in the day's bright light,
I hear the giggles of delight.
What comes next is yet to find,
Maybe broccoli, or ice cream blind?

A compass points to lands unknown,
But first, I need to find my phone.
Will I forget to change my socks?
Or will I rule these garden rocks?

The sun is low, the jokes are high,
A squirrel just winked, I swear, oh my!
With every shadow, a chance to play,
In this wide world, come what may.

Tomorrow's funny, it gives me glee,
To tumble through life, wild and free.
Let laughter reign, let worries stall,
As we chase together, the horizon's call.

Whispers of What's to Come

In the morning light, a cat sings,
Balancing dreams on cartoon wings.
Chickens plotting world takeover,
While I sip tea, feeling quite clever.

Through the clouds, a snail zooms fast,
Waving at clouds that never last.
Tomorrow's secrets tucked away,
Like socks that vanish on laundry day.

Pants on backwards is the style,
Here to stay for quite a while.
A dance parade on sidewalks wide,
With rubber ducks that take a ride.

Giggling ghosts with silly hats,
Mimicking all the local cats.
Whispers float on breezy sails,
Of future tales and birthday fails.

A Glimpse of Possibilities

A squirrel in shades, plotting his next heist,
While pigeons argue, laughing so precise.
The toaster pops, unleashing crumbs,
Singing songs of breakfast drums.

In the garden, a gnome wears bling,
Confidently swaying, doing his thing.
Tomorrow's plans may seem absurd,
Like talking onions, watching birds.

Dancing socks and vibrant shoes,
Chasing rainbows where logic snooze.
A fruitcake that dreams it's a star,
Wants to tour in a candy car.

Under a mushroom umbrella, they sit,
Nibbling giggles, oh what a hit!
Tomorrow's tricks are worth a glance,
With silly hats and a frog's romance.

Reflections of a New Day

Mirror, mirror, what do you see?
A dancing llama, wild and free.
With socks that twinkle and a grin so wide,
Every stumble is a joyride.

Banana phones blasting tunes,
Sending messages to fluffy loons.
In pajamas, a parade of dreams,
Riding on laughter, or so it seems.

Coffee frogs leap to the bar,
Planning a party with cookie jars.
Tomorrow's fate, a game of chance,
Where jellies hop and pickles dance.

Waking up with a raucous cheer,
Gags and giggles filling the air.
As the sun peeks with a grin so bright,
We'll paint the skies a comical light.

Through the Veil of Time

Tick-tock, the clock gets wise,
With every tick, it tells us lies.
A rabbit wearing a hat so grand,
Promises tricks from a magic hand.

Invisible bunnies race on walls,
While pasta noodles bounce and crawl.
The future's full of silly views,
Like mismatched socks and runaway shoes.

A time machine made of bubblegum,
Squeezed with giggles and lots of fun.
Tomorrow's news is a cheeky charade,
With meaty jokes and lemonade.

From yesteryears, the fish all talk,
In whispers grand, they take a walk.
Within the jest and silly rhyme,
Lies a future bouncy and sublime.

Kaleidoscope of New Beginnings

Colors dance and shift so bright,
A jester's hat in morning light.
Donuts sprout from pots of gold,
Wacky stories yet untold.

Chickens fly, the sky's a joke,
Lemonade rivers, bubbles poke.
Llamas laughing in a race,
Tomorrow's fun, a wacky place.

Through the Looking Glass of Time

Ticking clocks that run awry,
Cats in top hats whisper, 'Hi!'
Jumping beans begin to sing,
Nonsense rules, oh what a fling!

Mirrors crack with silly grins,
Marshmallow clouds and fish in bins.
Every second's just a laugh,
In this dreamy, quirky path.

The Rising Dawn

Sunshine spills like jellybeans,
Bouncing frogs and silly scenes.
Toast with faces grins at me,
Peanut butter trees are free!

Cereal rains from fields up high,
Giggling squirrels all fly by.
In the morning's blushing spree,
Laughter's here, it's plain to see!

Constellations of Future Dreams

Stars that wink and swish around,
Silly wishes in the sound.
Pickles flying, chasing cheese,
Dancing onions in the breeze.

Galaxies of giggles bloom,
Toot the horn, make room for room!
Asteroids with fluffy tails,
Laughing loudly as they sail.

Untamed Futures

In a world where socks don't match,
Cats ride bikes, making quite the catch.
Pigeons wear hats, quite the sight,
Llamas in suits, ready for a flight.

Breakfast is served on a skateboard,
With toast that sings, quite adored.
Jellybeans grow on trees so tall,
Who needs a fortune when you have a ball?

Rainbows dance in silly shoes,
Waffles that giggle, just for a snooze.
Time skips like stones on a lake,
Building castles made of cake.

Oh! The surprises that await,
In wild dreams where fun can't wait.
Tomorrow may hold wonders untold,
Just grab your hat; be brave, be bold!

Light Beyond the Curtain

Behind the drapes, a parade of jesters,
Squirrels in tutus, the wild investors.
Cookies talk gossip, share a few laughs,
While lemonade dreams float on bubble baths.

A pickle plays piano, oh what a tune!
Dancing with dust bunnies beneath the moon.
Banana peels slip, but who really minds?
Laughter escapes like some magical winds.

Unicorns trip over glittery trails,
While jellybeans sail on chocolate gales.
Peeking through curtains brings giggles in heaps,
Tomorrow's secrets are silly, it peeps.

So raise a toast to the light you can see,
In the quirkiest dreams, come join the spree!
With whimsy and wonder, let it all glide,
In a fit of laughter, let joy be your ride!

Fragments of Tomorrow's Canvas

Brush strokes of laughter, colors that brawl,
Art made from socks, the finest of all.
Doodles of fish wearing top hats and ties,
Creating a ruckus, they dance in the skies.

Paint spills like jelly on toast made for glee,
Running in circles, a party for three.
Crayons debate, which one's the best,
While play-dough dreams take a colorful rest.

Tomorrow's a canvas, splattered with cheer,
With marshmallows flying and cupcakes adrift here.
Let the brushes twirl, let the colors collide,
In this mixed-up world where laughter can't hide.

So grab a palette, join the mad race,
Make art that tickles, that giggles in space.
Fragments of fun in a kaleidoscope dance,
In tomorrow's embrace, let's give it a chance!

Opening to the Unknown

An odd little door swings open with squeaks,
Blowing confetti and giggling geeks.
Out tumble creatures, all zany and bright,
Wearing pajamas, what a silly sight!

Toasters are toasting the news of the day,
While spoons throw a party, come join the fray.
Cats in top hats juggle feathers and beans,
As rain falls like syrup on candy machines.

Open your heart to the wild and absurd,
Where marshmallow clouds dance, unperturbed.
Jump into whimsy, let laughter ignite,
In the land of nonsense, such sweet delight!

It's here in the chaos that joy can be found,
Through the air of the quirky, magenta profound.
Come one, come all, to the carnival show,
Opening doors to the unknown, let it flow!

Glimpses Beneath the Curtain

Peeking through the cloth of fate,
I saw a cat that danced late.
It tripped on dreams, fell on a shoe,
And laughed as if it always knew.

The future giggles from afar,
Waving arms like a new-born star.
A squirrel in pajamas strikes a pose,
While the moon just giggles at its clothes.

Tickling toes of passing clouds,
Their laughter echoes, bright and loud.
They paint the sky with whipped cream swirls,
And sprinkle it with happy curls.

So why not join this frolicsome dance?
Life's a circus, just take a chance.
With quirks and giggles, we'll pave the way,
Into tomorrow's jolly play.

Shielding the Dawn of Change

Behind the glass, a pancake flips,
A sunrise made with breakfast quips.
Eggs do the cha-cha on the plate,
While toast shouts, "Just you wait, just wait!"

The clock ticks backward, what a sight,
As socks and shoes hold a pillow fight.
The sun decides to take a nap,
While shadows dance beneath a cap.

Jellybeans march with a jolly beat,
To wake the world from cozy sleep.
They shout, "Let's sprout; let's make a scene!"
With glitter clouds and peppermint green.

So peek beyond this everyday stage,
Where ticklish dreams play in a cage.
Laughing clouds weave tales anew,
As we discover the funny hue.

Out of Focus, Into Clarity

A foggy lens, a blurry sight,
A fish in a hat played peek-a-light.
It juggled bubbles, floated by,
While giggling birds began to fly.

In funny frames, my world is skewed,
Cats in tutus, tea with food.
Lemonade rivers flow with cheer,
As sprinkles rain from the bright smear.

Mixing colors, life's a paint,
A bumblebee hums, claiming saint.
He tripped on petals, fell on grass,
Sipping honey from a glass.

Take a gander, adjust the lens,
See nutty critters as your friends.
In every blur, a giggle waits,
Just wriggle free from the tedious fates.

Breathtaking Horizons Beyond

A pogo stick that bounces high,
With a rainbow tied to the sky.
A porcupine sporting a flair,
Nudges the sun, spins in mid-air.

The horizon dances, waves a cheer,
As jellyfish join in from the pier.
They ride the waves on lollipop boats,
Singing tunes with sweet little notes.

Polka dots shout from mountains tall,
While koalas in shades enjoy the call.
Their laughter trickles through the trees,
And fills the air with silly tease.

So lift your head and join the fun,
In every corner, joy has spun.
A world of giggles waits to see,
The breathtaking sights of glee and glee.

Into the Unknown Canvas

A blank sheet stares, like an empty plate,
As I ponder colors that might seem great.
I trip on the brush, it flies through the air,
Painting my ceiling—a masterpiece rare!

The cat jumps in, with paws full of paint,
Now my art's a crime, so I can't complain.
The walls are all yellow, my floors are now blue,
And my shoes? Oh dear, they are a colorful zoo!

With each splash, I giggle, and laughter unfolds,
As the chaos of color my sanity holds.
Someday I'll frame this, and hang it up high,
For in perfect madness, my dreams touch the sky!

So here's to the mess, and here's to the fun,
Creating a world where laughter gets spun.
Tomorrow's a canvas, for who knows what's found,
I'll dance as I paint, while the paint's swirling 'round!

The Bridge to What is Yet

I built a bridge made of bubblegum sticks,
Bouncing across, I ignore little tricks.
The trolls are all busy, they're dancing in pairs,
While I wave my arms, only causing made flares!

I skip and I hop, the bridge starts to sway,
Rubber bands stretch as I giggle and play.
'What's on the other side?' I squeal with delight,
A land filled with snacks and a fountain of Sprite!

But wait! What's that? A giant made of cheese?
I chase after crumbs, feeling light as a breeze.
He laughs, then he rolls, and I'm rolling too,
In this silly adventure where dreams come true!

So come join my journey, let's laugh all the way,
We'll skip on the bridge, let our worries decay.
What waits on the other side, we just can't tell,
But with giggles and glee, who needs it so well?

Morning's Promise Awaits

The rooster squawks like a broken alarm,
As I stare at the sun, I might just do harm.
Socks on my hands, and cereal for shoes,
At breakfast menu, I'll gladly refuse!

The toast pops up like a circus of bread,
My coffee spills out, and then paints the spread.
The cat steals my bacon, with stealth like a pro,
A feline's ambitions on full morning show!

So I make them a deal, a buttered delight,
"One for you, one for me!"—but I shan't get it right.
For every bite taken, I laugh at my fate,
In this morning madness, I'm feeling so great!

So here's to the breakfast with quirks galore,
When morning's a canvas, and chaos's in store.
With giggles and crumbs still stuck to my face,
Each dawn is a promise; let's savor the chase!

Beyond the Glass

Through panes we gaze, what do we see?
A cat in a hat, or maybe a bee?
The sky is a canvas, painted with glee,
And squirrels play chess, oh the joy, oh the spree!

A dog in a suit, struts down the lane,
Delighted in raindrops, he dances with rain.
Trees wear their coats of bright green, it's plain,
While clouds tickle rooftops with gentle refrain.

A fish in the air, is it really a dream?
Or just what you see when you're lost in the beam?
The future's a riddle, or so it might seem,
With laughter and whimsy, life flows like a stream.

So peek through the glass, let your worries take flight,
In this quirky world, every day feels just right.
For who knows tomorrow, or what brings delight?
Let's giggle together, from morning to night!

Echoes of the Dawn

Awake from our slumber, the sun starts to glow,
A rooster in slippers, puts on quite a show.
With socks on his feet, he's ready to crow,
While coffee's brewing, oh what a flow!

The clock strikes a tune, it's chicken disco,
Dancing on tables, they're putting on a show.
Toast jumps in the air, with butter you know,
Breakfast is wild, it's a culinary throw!

Birds chirp in chorus, with melodies bright,
A squirrel in a cape, he takes off in flight.
The flowers all giggle, with colors so light,
The dawn is our canvas, oh what a sight!

As shadows retreat from their nighttime retreat,
Laughter fills spaces, it's a wonderful feat.
Embrace the new day, let it sweep you off your feet,
For echoes of dawn are a whimsical treat!

Horizons Unseen

Peeking beyond where the grass meets the sky,
I see a parade of fish learning to fly.
They twirl in the air, oh my, oh me, why?
A kite-eating tree lets out a big sigh.

Jellybeans rain from clouds made of fluff,
They're sweeter than dreams, oh isn't that tough?
Sailing on spoons feels a bit too rough,
But life's all about that unpredictable stuff!

So grab your umbrella, it's candy that falls,
While penguins in tuxedos attend grandiose balls.
The sun cracks a joke, and the moon just enthralls,
Horizons unseen, where the laughter just calls.

With giggles as fuel, and joy as our guide,
Adventure awaits on this whimsical ride.
For life's a grand story, with each turn and slide,
So let's cherish these moments, with hearts open wide!

Veil of Future Light

Behind every laughter, a secret unfurls,
With frogs in bow ties, and twirls in the swirls.
They leap from the pond, making vapor trails twirl,
And whisper of wonders that life gently hurls.

Through a curtain of giggles, I spy a bright mouse,
Who's painting the ceilings of this dreamy house.
With colors that shimmer, it's hard to espouse,
A tapestry woven, no boring spouse!

A robot named Bobo, serving ice cream cones,
Drops scoops on the floor, saying "Oops, I'm alone!"
He dances through chaos, in happy warm tones,
While cats in pajamas discuss ancient bones.

The veil of bright futures, with laughter and cheer,
Prompts moments so silly, they draw us all near.
In a world filled with wonder, let's live without fear,
For joy is our compass, let's make that quite clear!

Discovery Beyond the Pane

Peering out, I see a cat,
Wearing boots and a cool hat.
He leaps from the fence with flair,
Chasing shadows through the air.

A squirrel with a tiny drum,
Marches by, oh what a bum!
With every beat, he sings a tale,
Of nuts and dreams on a grand scale.

The clouds are dancing in a line,
Waltzing clouds, it's quite divine!
They march and prance, they twirl and spin,
Even they see where fun begins.

A flower waves, its petals bright,
Sprays confetti, what a sight!
Nature's party, so surreal,
Through the glass, I feel the squeal!

Views Beyond the Present

A chicken in a tuxedo stands,
Holding a mic with little hands.
He croons a tune, so silly and spry,
Making the cows just laugh and sigh.

A marshmallow cloud floats on by,
It's fluffier than a pie in the sky.
Next to it, a rainbow rides a bike,
Pedaling hard, oh what a hike!

Llama in shades sips iced tea,
Saying, "Oh, just wait and see!"
The sun's got jokes, it winks and glows,
Time for laughter, that's how it goes.

A frog in a bowtie leaps with glee,
Telling jokes, oh can't you see?
Through the glass, such quirky sights,
Bringing smiles on sunny nights!

The Promise in the Air

A balloon tied up with a string,
Bounces high, oh joy it brings.
Whispers secrets to the breeze,
Telling tales among the trees.

Butterflies play hopscotch, oh my!
Counting clouds that float on high.
Game of tag with the bumblebee,
Every flip is pure glee.

The sun is grinning, can you tell?
Playing tricks, casting a spell.
It wears a hat made of rays,
Illuminating silly ways.

A parrot speaks with a laugh,
Charts the path to fun by a graph.
Through the air, the giggles soar,
Every moment, let's explore!

Anticipation at the Threshold

At the door, a penguin waits,
Tapping feet, he anticipates.
In his flipper, he holds a snack,
"Join me for fun!" he quips with a whack.

A giraffe swings in, rocking slow,
His neck a sight with quite the show.
With every sway, he wears a grin,
Inviting all to jump right in!

The clock ticks loud like a drum,
Time for silliness, here it comes!
So gather 'round, don't be shy,
Funny moments never fly by.

A raccoon pops up with a wink,
Spreading joy as quick as a blink.
Through anticipation, we'll all partake,
A celebration for laughter's sake!

Threads of Potential Weaved

In a room with a cat on the chair,
I ponder visions beyond my hair.
With colors splashed in all the wrong places,
I giggle at life's odd, silly faces.

Juggling dreams like a clown in flight,
Each one bounces, a balloon in the night.
Tangled yarns of my best-made schemes,
Pulling laughter from the wildest dreams.

In tangled thoughts, I sew and twine,
Creating futures with mischief divine.
Stitching tomorrow with threads of cheer,
Frolicing futures, come join the sphere!

With a twist and a turn, the fabric blends,
All my worries, laughter, and friends.
Who knew this yarn would fray, unwind?
A patchwork quilt of the funniest kind!

Beyond the Shadows' Edge

At the crack of dawn, my shadow jokes,
Whispers of light, oh how it pokes!
Dancing shadows with no real aim,
Playing a hide-and-seek kind of game.

Beneath a sunbeam, a quick little twist,
Did I just see a shadow on the list?
I chase it down like a rogue balloon,
Catching giggles before the day's noon.

With a belly laugh, I hop on a tune,
The shadows join in, making mischief soon.
And all those worries, they trip and fall,
As we dance and frolic, feeling quite small.

Every hop is a bright surprise,
A silly waltz beneath open skies.
Beyond the edge, where the silliness thrives,
We gather our dreams, oh, how it drives!

Signs of a New Dawn

Silly roosters sing songs off-key,
Telling the world it's time for tea!
With a wink and nudge, they strut and boast,
Claiming breakfast as their proud toast!

Sunrise giggles burst with light,
Each beam a chuckle, fate feels bright.
The clouds wear glasses, a bright new style,
Making rainbows laugh with every mile.

In this morning that tickles the soul,
Grass blades wiggle towards their goal.
Each drop of dew shines with delight,
A comedic spark on a humorous flight.

So let's embrace this quirky dawn,
With hats and shoes all mismatched and drawn.
For signs of joy are all around,
In the ticklish laughter of the morning sound!

Mapping Tomorrow's Dreams

With a map drawn in crayon and glee,
I plan my travels, no rules for me!
Through chocolate rivers and jellybean hills,
Where laughter flows, and joy fulfills.

Each route leads to the silliest sights,
A land of socks and scruffy delights.
Where every corner blooms with surprise,
And giggles are hidden in the skies.

Pin the tail on fortune, embrace the chase,
With silly antics and a crazy pace.
We'll dance through moments with chuckles in mind,
For treasure's found in the silly we find.

So let's pack our dreams in gumdrop bags,
Map out our whims, forget the drags.
For tomorrow awaits with a comical scene,
In the wildest adventures we've ever dreamed!

Threads of Time and Space

In a world where time is a rubber band,
Things can twist in ways we don't understand.
Yesterday's soup is tomorrow's delight,
You might wake up dancing in the middle of night.

Cats wear hats, and dogs can sing,
Rabbits ride bikes; it's a curious thing.
The clock's tick-tock is a silly dance,
As we weave through futures with a laugh and a chance.

Space is a jester with tricks up its sleeve,
The stars play tag when we dare to believe.
Comets throw parties, and black holes play peek,
In this zany universe, the laughter is sleek.

So let's spin our yarns and brighten the day,
With colors and whims that lead us astray.
For each thread we pull pulls us closer to fun,
In this tapestry woven, we've only just begun.

Forecast of Hope

The weatherman's hat is askew on his head,
He's predicting a party, but we're all misled.
A sprinkle of giggles, a drizzle of cheer,
With a chance of ice cream floating near.

Raindrops in rainbow, they dance down the street,
Each puddle a mirror where silly dreams meet.
Umbrellas are hats in this drizzly delight,
Where laughter and joy carry us through the night.

Tomorrow's a blank page, a canvas to paint,
With crayons of fortune, let's not be quaint.
A forecast of fun, it won't rain on our spree,
Every cloud has a giggle, just wait and see!

So grab your galoshes, let's splash in the sun,
For this crazy adventure has only begun.
With tickles from breezes and sunshine's embrace,
We'll weather each storm with a smile on our face.

The Unfolding Horizon

Horizons are folding like origami dreams,
With paper cranes soaring on whimsical beams.
Each crease a new path, each fold a new laugh,
What a ridiculous way to draw up a graph!

Mountains are giggling, they wiggle and shake,
The valleys are chuckling at every mistake.
We'll climb to the peak of a slippery slope,
As we bounce through the air with unbridled hope.

The sun wears a grin like a Cheshire cat,
While clouds toss confetti; imagine that!
Stars twinkle wildly, they can barely contain,
The joy of this journey, the laughter, the gain.

So let's run with abandon into tomorrow,
Kicking up daisies, not worried of sorrow.
With horizons unfolding in skies painted gold,
It's a tapestry woven where adventures unfold.

Echoes of the Unseen

In shadows that giggle, secrets reside,
With whispers of mischief, they dance and they slide.
Echoes are laughing from corners unknown,
As they play hide-and-seek with the light that has shone.

The past throws a party, no RSVP,
You can slip through the doorway, come join the free.
Bubbles of time float like fish in a stream,
While the unseen flutters, uniquely supreme.

Listen for chuckles behind every door,
Doors that lead nowhere, but always to more.
A time-traveling snail with a monocle rests,
Counting the moments, it jestfully tests.

So let's jump right in, to see what we've missed,
In echoes of laughter, we can't help but twist.
With a wink from the universe, we'll roll with the flow,
For the unseen's revealed in the heart of the show.

Whirlwinds of Potential

In a house of sighs, a cat takes flight,
Chasing dust bunnies that twirl in light.
A coffee cup spills, but that's just fine,
We'll lap it up later, it's all divine.

The toaster dances with a gleeful pop,
Burnt toast confetti, it doesn't stop.
The fridge hums loud like a band gone wild,
While veggies dream of a parade, unfiled.

A sock slides in, joins the living room waltz,
Three-legged table joins, it's all a farce.
As laughter spills like milk on the floor,
We chase the future through an open door.

With every tumble, hope takes a chance,
The world's a circus, and we'll all dance.
The whirlwind spins, our fun's a must,
In tomorrows bright, we leap with trust.

Lanterns for the Future

Balloons float high, tied to dreams of gold,
Mischief awaits like stories told.
An old man chuckles with a wink and nod,
As jellybeans bounce, they leave us awed.

Crayons escape from a box at night,
Drawing futures under the moonlight bright.
A shoe gets a party with a polka dot,
While spaghetti slurps, oh, what a plot!

In gardens we giggle at sunflowers swaying,
Who knew plants had such fine ballet playing?
The squirrels make bets on the acorn race,
As we twirl in joy, a wild embrace.

Futures made of candy and glee,
Glance at the lanterns, come dance with me!
We'll light up paths with our silly song,
In this land of whimsy, we all belong.

Subtle Shifts in Light

The sun peeks in with a cheeky grin,
Painting shadows where giggles begin.
A table of muffins, a race to the end,
We'll fight for the sprinkles, my sugary friend!

Curtains flutter as if they could talk,
Whispering secrets with a wink and a walk.
The fridge hums a tune like a disco ball,
Join in the chorus, we've got a call!

The mirror winks back, oh, what a tease,
Reflecting our dreams with incredible ease.
A sock puppet sings, the audience roars,
As laughter dances right out of our doors.

With every soft flicker, the future unfolds,
In a playpen of laughter, where joy is bold.
Through every bright window, the spirit takes flight,
Chasing tomorrow, with love and delight.

Embracing Tomorrow's Dream

An umbrella opens in the middle of cheer,
Revealing a dance-off for all to hear.
With mismatched shoes, we all take a stand,
Dancing in puddles, as per our plan!

A butterfly winks at a puzzled old shoe,
"Let's flutter together and see what's new!"
The clock strikes fun, as the seconds rewind,
Creating mischief that's quite well-designed.

Between giggles and glances, the grass starts to hum,
While jellybeans tumble, saying "We've come!"
With daisies in hand and laughter that beams,
We hug the ridiculous, embrace our dreams.

So come, take a leap into the absurd,
Where futures are woven in whimsy—a word!
We'll dance through the chaos, with smiles as our guide,
In this carnival of spirits, let's run with pride!

Foresight in Stillness

In a chair, the cat sits tight,
Staring at shadows, plotting flight.
With a twitchy tail, time ticks slow,
Contemplating where the mice might go.

A squirrel spied through glass so clear,
Wonders if it could make the leap here.
Suppose it dreams of jumping high,
While I just dream of a piece of pie.

Chasing Distant Glimmers

A firefly darts across the night,
Can it see my puzzled fright?
Is it just a dot of light?
Or a beacon saying, 'Hang tight'?

The moon winks down with playful glee,
Blast off! Let's play hide-and-seek, you see.
As stars giggle and begin to dance,
I trip on dreams, must take a chance.

Between Now and Next

The toaster pops, it's time to toast,
Yet here I am, a sleepy ghost.
Maybe tomorrow, I'll jump in line,
For now, who wants a snack divine?

Clock hands race; what a silly game,
Next is here, and I'm still the same.
A dance to shuffle, a leap with flair,
I'll grab a biscuit while I stare.

A Glimpse Through Change

A comical bird in a funny hat,
Sits on a fence, proud as a brat.
It caws at change with a confident tone,
"I'll fly tomorrow, but today I'm home!"

As seasons swirl in a colorful blaze,
I gaze out, lost in a hedgehog's maze.
Underneath my window, a garden grows,
With plants that dance like a Broadway show.

Windowsill Whispers

A cat sits perched, spying on the street,
Dreaming of birds that are quick on their feet.
A fly buzzes by, teasing with glee,
While the dog barks loud, trying to flee.

In bright daylight, the plants stretch and yawn,
Dancing in sunshine, from dusk till dawn.
A squirrel stops by, gives a cheeky grin,
And shouts, "Hey, human! Let the games begin!"

On this sill, secrets are laughing away,
As dust motes twirl in a whimsical ballet.
The world outside, it's a circus of fun,
Who knew a windowsill could outshine the sun?

With every glance, the drama unfolds,
A tale of mischief that never grows old.
Oh what a view, it's a comedy show,
Right here on the sill, where the laughter will flow.

Shades of What Awaits

The curtains flutter, a breeze starts to play,
As shadows dance lightly, in bright disarray.
A rabbit hops by, in a madcap chase,
While a plant quietly smirks, in its leafy embrace.

Peeking through, what a sight to behold,
A mailman slips, as the mailbox grows bold.
With packages tumbling, like clowns from a car,
The morning unfolds like a wacky sitar.

Rain clouds gather, with giggles in tow,
They tumble and rumble, putting on a show.
But then comes the sun, with a wink and a grin,
Throwing shadows like games, let the laughter begin!

Each moment so silly, no weight on the mind,
In this quirky landscape, humor we find.
For every shade dancing, holds joy in its light,
Through laughter and sunshine, we dare take flight.

Through the Frame of Hope

Watching the world through a gleaming pane,
Each giggle and stumble is hard to contain.
A toddler trips, and oh what a sound,
As ducks quack along, they just can't be found!

Through this frame, a parade of delight,
Of joggers who trip and dogs in full flight.
A neighbor's old lawn chair makes its grand fall,
While someone yells, "Oops! That was not my call!"

A breeze flutters by with a tickle and tease,
Whispers of mishaps dance through the trees.
The world outside is a carnival bright,
With funny little moments that spring to life right.

Each frame tells a story, each glance holds a gleam,
In a bonkers bazaar, where laughter can beam.
So peek through the glass, let your spirit unwind,
For joy is the treasure that's witty and kind.

Dawn's Invitation

Awake to the chirps, a delightfully loud crew,
As morning unfolds in a dazzling view.
A squirrel drops acorns, with quite the flair,
Creating a ruckus, no moment to spare.

The sun peeks in, with a goofy bright face,
Baking the world in a warm, golden embrace.
While the cat on the sill bends with a yawn,
Contemplating whether today's worth the dawn.

Breakfast gets made, and chaos ensues,
As a pancake flips high, accusing the blues.
With forks in the air and syrup on cats,
Each mishap is met with some hearty laughs!

Through windows of morning, oh what a delight,
Life's little antics bring everyone light.
So gather the giggles; let the fun unfurl,
For the promise of laughter is a wonderful pearl!

The Promise of Change

The clock ticks loudly, oh what a sound,
Time slips away, where's the lost found?
A cat in a hat, juggling a pea,
Promises change, like a bird in a tree.

Pants on the floor, a sock on the wall,
Dancing in circles, we're having a ball.
Lemonade rivers, with fish wearing coats,
Now that's a change, as fun as it floats!

A shoe full of pudding, oh what a feast,
Tomorrow we'll laugh, not worried in the least.
Pies in the sky, they'll come down for tea,
Change is just laughter, you wait and you see!

So let's embrace wobbly chairs and wild hats,
Funny little surprises, let's all raise our bats.
The promise of giggles, let's open the door,
With a whoosh and a carry, we'll frolic once more!

Illumination Ahead

Lights are a-dimming, but the fun's just begun,
With glow-in-the-dark jellybeans, we're number one!
Our shadows are dancing, they twist and they bend,
In a symphony of silliness, the laughter won't end.

A toaster is singing, the kettle has shoes,
In a world upside down, it's all silly news.
As stars wear top hats and planets play chess,
Every bright corner's a chance to impress.

So here comes the sunshine, it's strumming a tune,
While squirrels in bowties are dancing like loons.
Illumination is laughter, a sparkly light,
In this whimsical world, everything's just right!

So grab your umbrellas, the rain sings a song,
Raining confetti and giggles along.
With each silly dance, we'll sparkle and play,
Illuminate the night, let's laugh all the way!

Routes Yet to Traverse

Maps made of candy, with paths lined in cheer,
Discovering giggles, with friends oh so near.
A frog in a bowler, sings 'Hop On My Back!'
Let's venture through silliness, down the giggle track.

Pickles in pajamas wander around,
Jellybean traffic, oh what a sound!
A river of giggles flows right through the park,
It'll lead us to fun, just follow the spark.

With bubbles for bridges, and donut-shaped moon,
We'll skip through the dreams, oh what a festoon!
Routes yet to traverse, in laughter we roam,
Every twist and each turn, leads us back home.

So pack up your smiles, it's time for a trip,
With carrot-lined roads, let's make our first skip.
Those funny adventures, we'll never regret,
For every new path, a new joke is met!

Shattered Boundaries

Who put the jelly on the ceiling so high?
With pancakes tumbling, I don't even know why.
The moon in a tutu, it's dancing with glee,
Those shattered boundaries, just let them be free!

Our walls are made of marshmallows and joy,
With bubble-wrap floors for each girl and each boy.
In a land where the grass is made out of cake,
We'll jump over giggles; make no mistake!

Breaking down borders with laughter so loud,
Flying on unicorns, oh we're so proud!
Each giggle a hammer, each laugh a new tool,
Shattered boundaries wrapped in the silliest rule.

So let's paint a rainbow with all of our quirks,
Dancing on rainbows, where silliness lurks.
Together in laughter, we'll build up our dream,
In this whimsical world, we're all part of the team!

Vista of tomorrow's Hearts

Peeking through the glass so clear,
Sights of future's quirks appear.
Socks mismatched, a dance so bright,
Laughing at the morning light.

Inverted hats and shoes on wrong,
Humor in a daily song.
A cat wears shades and struts with pride,
Chasing dreams where fun won't hide.

A pirate hat atop a broom,
Creation springs; it's pure cartoon.
Unicorns dance in the street,
While robots sway to a funky beat.

Juggling eggs, a breakfast dare,
Life's absurd with laughter rare.
Tomorrow calls with goofy glee,
A silly world for you and me.

Chasing the Unwritten Path

Adventures dance in endless fun,
Chasing dreams under the sun.
With pizza hats and bubblegum,
We run with glee, a silly drum.

Sidewalks twist like noodle soup,
Holding hands, we form a loop.
A giraffe rides on a skateboard,
Planning next week's circus hoard.

Backflips in a runaway cart,
We paint the sky; it's a work of art.
Plan? Who needs it? Life's a game,
With neon wigs, we flip the fame.

We chase the winds, the whimsy quest,
Finding joy in each jest.
A pie in my face, a soft embrace,
In the laughter, we find our place.

The Light of Possibility

Swinging between the beams of fun,
Chasing shadows, we outrun.
A robot sings with a silly grin,
In this world, where laughter wins.

Glasses made of jelly beans,
Pandas in polka dot jeans.
A game of hopscotch in the air,
Bouncing ideas everywhere.

Clouds are made of cotton candy,
Tickle monsters creeping handy.
An opera sung by raccoon bands,
Life's absurd in merry strands.

In this glow of endless play,
Each wild moment leads the way.
Forget the plans, just look around,
In laughter's light, new dreams are found.

Unraveling the Next Chapter

Pages flip in jolly haste,
Each word a treat, a tasty taste.
With pickle hats and funny toes,
Who knows where this story goes?

Pants on fire, but we're still cool,
Running fast, that's our rule.
Dancing ducks and cake that sings,
Life's a story filled with wings.

Twirling tales, ridiculous spins,
A giggle storm, let the fun begins.
Grab your friends; don't be late,
To the comedy of fate.

So let's unwrap each quirky line,
Fun awaits; it's so divine.
With laughter, charm, and a little flair,
Unravel the tale with joyful air.

Futures Unfurled

In a garden of dreams, we stand with glee,
Chasing bubbles that dance, wild and free.
A fortune teller says, "You'll wear a hat!"
I pray it's not one shaped like a cat!

The future's a jester, playing with fate,
Dancing on rooftops, we laugh at our weight.
Next Tuesday, I'm told, I might win the race,
But first, I must learn to tie my shoelace!

A bird in a wig chirps tunes from the sun,
While I search for my keys, it's all just great fun.
Tomorrow's a party with socks on our heads,
Let's jump on our bikes, wear pajamas instead!

So we toast to the future with mugs full of cheer,
And laugh at the thought of our greatest career.
Perhaps we'll be astronauts or simply just chefs,
Living our lives like it's all just a jest!

The Lattice of Dawn

Morning breaks softly, a giggle between,
Coffee spills over, what a silly scene!
The toaster's a dancer, popping with flair,
Oh look, there's my breakfast! It's gone—where's a chair?

In a world made of waffles, syrupy streams,
I sail on a pancake, chasing my dreams.
Tomorrow they say I'll invent a loud song,
But for now, I'm just wondering where I belong!

The sun winks at me through the curtains they tend,
Predicting that I'll become pineapple's friend.
Together we'll rule the most fruity brigade,
While I laugh at my sneakers, serenely displayed.

So let's gather our hopes in a cereal bowl,
With marshmallow dreams, let's ignite our soul!
The dawn may be funny, with quirks of its own,
Yet each day we find joy in the unknown!

Echoes of Potential

Bouncing like rubber, I hop through the day,
My future's a riddle, in a comical way.
Today I will mail myself to the moon,
But first, I'll just nap, I'll leave around noon!

A cat in a tux pretends to read fate,
Whiskers on point, he seems quite innate.
I hope he will share what's next on my lists,
But he just knows where all the catnip is!

With balloons tied to dreams, we float and we spin,
Tomorrow will surely bring laughter and grin.
I'll juggle my worries, hit targets with ease,
While riding a unicycle—pass me the keys!

Let's look toward the future, a clown on a quest,
With shoes way too big for the strides of the best.
Oh, what will we find wrapped up in surprise?
Just giggles and hiccups, oh, how time flies!

Beyond the Frame

Pictures of laughter hang on the wall,
A cat wearing glasses is having a ball.
I glimpse at tomorrow through this silly lens,
Where squirrels start waltzing, oh, what fun trends!

A banana in pajamas is taking a stroll,
Claiming the corner as part of its role.
Tomorrow's a party, full of odd toys,
Where bubbles are traded for giggles and joy!

The clock winks at me, with arms crossed just so,
"Not now!" I declare, "I'm busy with glow!"
Paint splashes echo dreams brightly untold,
As I paint my tomorrow with colors so bold.

So let's dance through our futures, each quick witted stride,
With fruit hats a-flying, we'll relish the ride.
Tomorrow's a canvas of silly delight,
Where laughter's the brush that makes all things bright!

The Path Unseen

Beneath the steps, the path may twist,
A rubber chicken's on the list!
Each turn holds jokes we've yet to find,
With giggles laced in every kind.

A squirrel in pants runs for his life,
He trips on roots, oh what a strife!
Laughter echoes through the trees,
As echoes tumble on the breeze.

An octopus on rollerblades,
Befriends a cat who serenades.
Through unseen trails, they brave the quest,
Creating chaos, not a rest!

So take the leap, don't hesitate,
For laughter waits and won't be late.
In paths unseen, let smiles reign,
With funny tales that break the chain.

Horizons Awaiting

A llama somersaults with flair,
While cats on surfboards catch some air.
Horizons stretch with silly dreams,
Where laughter flows in comet streams.

The sun paints smiles across blue skies,
As hedgehogs launch into surprise.
With every blink, a prank unfolds,
In places where the boldest go.

Shoelaces tied in knots so grand,
The puppy's leading, what a stand!
Through fields of giggles and delight,
They chase the clouds, a comical sight.

So look ahead; what joy awaits!
With puns and tales that elevate.
In horizons bright, let laughter play,
And turn the mundane into a ballet.

The Symphony of Tomorrow's Whispers

A kazoo band plays on the street,
As ants all dance to keep the beat.
With squeaky notes that lift the sun,
The symphony of joy's begun.

In gardens bright, the gnomes declare,
They'll start a band; just grab a chair!
A tuba's honk and trumpet's flare,
Turn silence into a wild affair.

The echoes of tomorrow's cheer,
Bring ducklings in a conga line near.
With every note, the laughter grows,
In this adventure nobody knows.

So let the whispers fill the air,
With joy and mischief everywhere.
The symphony sings out so clear,
Of funny moments, loud and dear!

Gardens of Untold Stories

In gardens lush, where snails recite,
With tales of cheese and moonlit flight.
Each flower's grin holds secrets rare,
Of sock puppets and kittens' flair.

A fruit bat juggles ripe bananas,
As hedgehogs spin in funny pianos.
With petals soft, they burst with glee,
Creating laughs as bright as can be.

In every corner, stories bloom,
Of frogs in capes and mice in rooms.
With every giggle, plants take wing,
To dance along and laugh and sing.

So wander through, let mirth unfurl,
In gardens rich, where laughter swirls.
With tales untold, let joy ignite,
And chase away the gloom of night.

www.ingramcontent.com/pod-product-compliance
Lightning Source LLC
Chambersburg PA
CBHW070006300426
43661CB00141B/252